THIS LUNCH PLANNER BELONGS TO:

_____

✉ _____

Please email me if you find this notebook

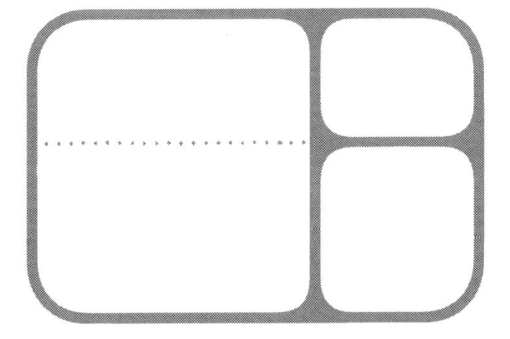

BENTGO FRESH

Get your lunchbox on AMAZON
www.ashleysnotebooks.com/BENTGO-FRESH

Copyright © 2019 by Ashley's Notebooks

All rights reserved. No part of this publication may be reproduced, distributed, or transmitted in any form or by any means, including photocopying, recording, or other electronic or mechanical methods, without the prior written permission of the publisher, except in the case of brief quotations embodied in critical reviews and certain other noncommercial uses permitted by copyright law. For permission requests, write to the publisher, addressed "Attention: Permissions Coordinator," at the address below.

info@ashleysnotebooks.com
www.ashleysnotebooks.com

school lunch
INSPIRATION

PROTEINS

- ○ turkey
- ○ ham
- ○ chicken
- ○ chickpeas
- ○ hummus
- ○ egg
- ○ yogourt
- ○ energy bites
- ○ meatballs
- ○ pepperoni
- ○ refried beans
- ○ nut butter
- ○ seed butter
- ○ Sliced lunchmeat
- ○ Blocks of cheese
- ○ Sliced cheese
- ○ Shredded cheese

FRUIT & VEG

- ○ apples
- ○ oranges
- ○ grapes
- ○ berries
- ○ watermelon
- ○ pears
- ○ apple sauce
- ○ raisins
- ○ plums
- ○ olives
- ○ cucumbers
- ○ carrots
- ○ sugar peas
- ○ carrots
- ○ celery
- ○ bell peppers
- ○ broccoli
- ○ lettuce
- ○ tomatoes

CARBS

- ○ bread
- ○ bagels
- ○ pita
- ○ tortilla
- ○ muffin
- ○ pancake
- ○ waffle
- ○ pasta
- ○ rice
- ○ crackers
- ○ pretzels
- ○ english muffin
- ○ roll
- ○ flatbread
- ○ potatoes
- ○ plantains
- ○ popcorn

SOMETHING FUN

- ○ chips
- ○ trail mix (with dark chocolate)
- ○ animal crackers
- ○ chocolate almonds
- ○ veggies straws
- ○ fruit leather
- ○ granola bar

lunch notes

Have a good day!	We love you!	You are a superstar!	YOU CAN DO IT!
Have a nice monday!	Today is tuesday	Have a nice wednesday!	Good thursday!
Hurra it is FRIDAY	Today is a beautiful day!	I am proud of you!	You are the best!

FREE PDF DOWNLOAD
www.ashleysnotebooks.com/lunch-notes

weekly

monday

○ Proteins ○ Carbs
○ Fruit & Veg ○ Fun

Snacks
_____
_____

Beverage
_____
_____

Rating ☆ ☆ ☆ ☆ ☆

tuesday

○ Proteins ○ Carbs
○ Fruit & Veg ○ Fun

Snacks
_____
_____

Beverage
_____
_____

Rating ☆ ☆ ☆ ☆ ☆

wednesday

○ Proteins ○ Carbs
○ Fruit & Veg ○ Fun

Snacks
_____
_____

Beverage
_____
_____

Rating ☆ ☆ ☆ ☆ ☆

lunch planner
FOR KIDS

thursday

○ Proteins ○ Carbs
○ Fruit & Veg ○ Fun

Snacks

Beverage

Rating ☆ ☆ ☆ ☆ ☆

friday

○ Proteins ○ Carbs
○ Fruit & Veg ○ Fun

Snacks

Beverage

Rating ☆ ☆ ☆ ☆ ☆

Favorites

Humm, please no more!

weekly

monday

○ Proteins ○ Carbs
○ Fruit & Veg ○ Fun

Snacks
_____
_____

Beverage
_____
_____

Rating ☆☆☆☆☆

tuesday

○ Proteins ○ Carbs
○ Fruit & Veg ○ Fun

Snacks
_____
_____

Beverage
_____
_____

Rating ☆☆☆☆☆

wednesday

○ Proteins ○ Carbs
○ Fruit & Veg ○ Fun

Snacks
_____
_____

Beverage
_____
_____

Rating ☆☆☆☆☆

lunch planner
FOR KIDS

thursday

- ○ Proteins   ○ Carbs
- ○ Fruit & Veg   ○ Fun

Snacks
_____
_____

Beverage
_____
_____

Rating ☆ ☆ ☆ ☆ ☆

friday

- ○ Proteins   ○ Carbs
- ○ Fruit & Veg   ○ Fun

Snacks
_____
_____

Beverage
_____
_____

Rating ☆ ☆ ☆ ☆ ☆

Favorites

Humm, please no more!

weekly

monday

○ Proteins   ○ Carbs
○ Fruit & Veg   ○ Fun

Snacks
_____
_____

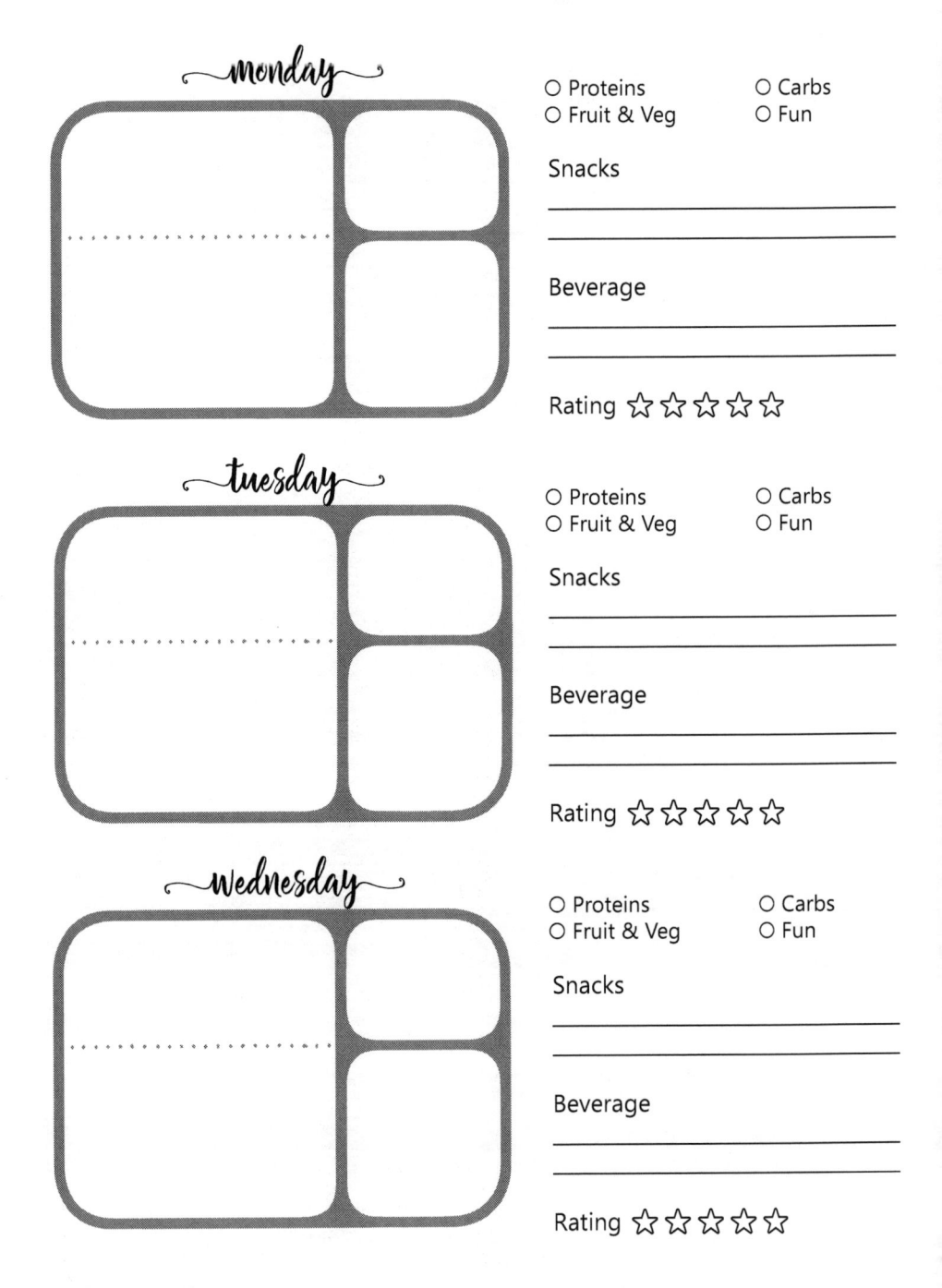

Beverage
_____
_____

Rating ☆ ☆ ☆ ☆ ☆

tuesday

○ Proteins   ○ Carbs
○ Fruit & Veg   ○ Fun

Snacks
_____
_____

Beverage
_____
_____

Rating ☆ ☆ ☆ ☆ ☆

wednesday

○ Proteins   ○ Carbs
○ Fruit & Veg   ○ Fun

Snacks
_____
_____

Beverage
_____
_____

Rating ☆ ☆ ☆ ☆ ☆

lunch planner
FOR KIDS

thursday

○ Proteins   ○ Carbs
○ Fruit & Veg   ○ Fun

Snacks

Beverage

Rating ☆ ☆ ☆ ☆ ☆

friday

○ Proteins   ○ Carbs
○ Fruit & Veg   ○ Fun

Snacks

Beverage

Rating ☆ ☆ ☆ ☆ ☆

Favorites

Humm, please no more!

Weekly

monday

○ Proteins   ○ Carbs
○ Fruit & Veg   ○ Fun

Snacks
_____
_____

Beverage
_____
_____

Rating ☆ ☆ ☆ ☆ ☆

tuesday

○ Proteins   ○ Carbs
○ Fruit & Veg   ○ Fun

Snacks
_____
_____

Beverage
_____
_____

Rating ☆ ☆ ☆ ☆ ☆

wednesday

○ Proteins   ○ Carbs
○ Fruit & Veg   ○ Fun

Snacks
_____
_____

Beverage
_____
_____

Rating ☆ ☆ ☆ ☆ ☆

lunch planner
FOR KIDS

thursday

○ Proteins ○ Carbs
○ Fruit & Veg ○ Fun

Snacks

Beverage

Rating ☆ ☆ ☆ ☆ ☆

friday

○ Proteins ○ Carbs
○ Fruit & Veg ○ Fun

Snacks

Beverage

Rating ☆ ☆ ☆ ☆ ☆

Favorites

Humm, please no more!

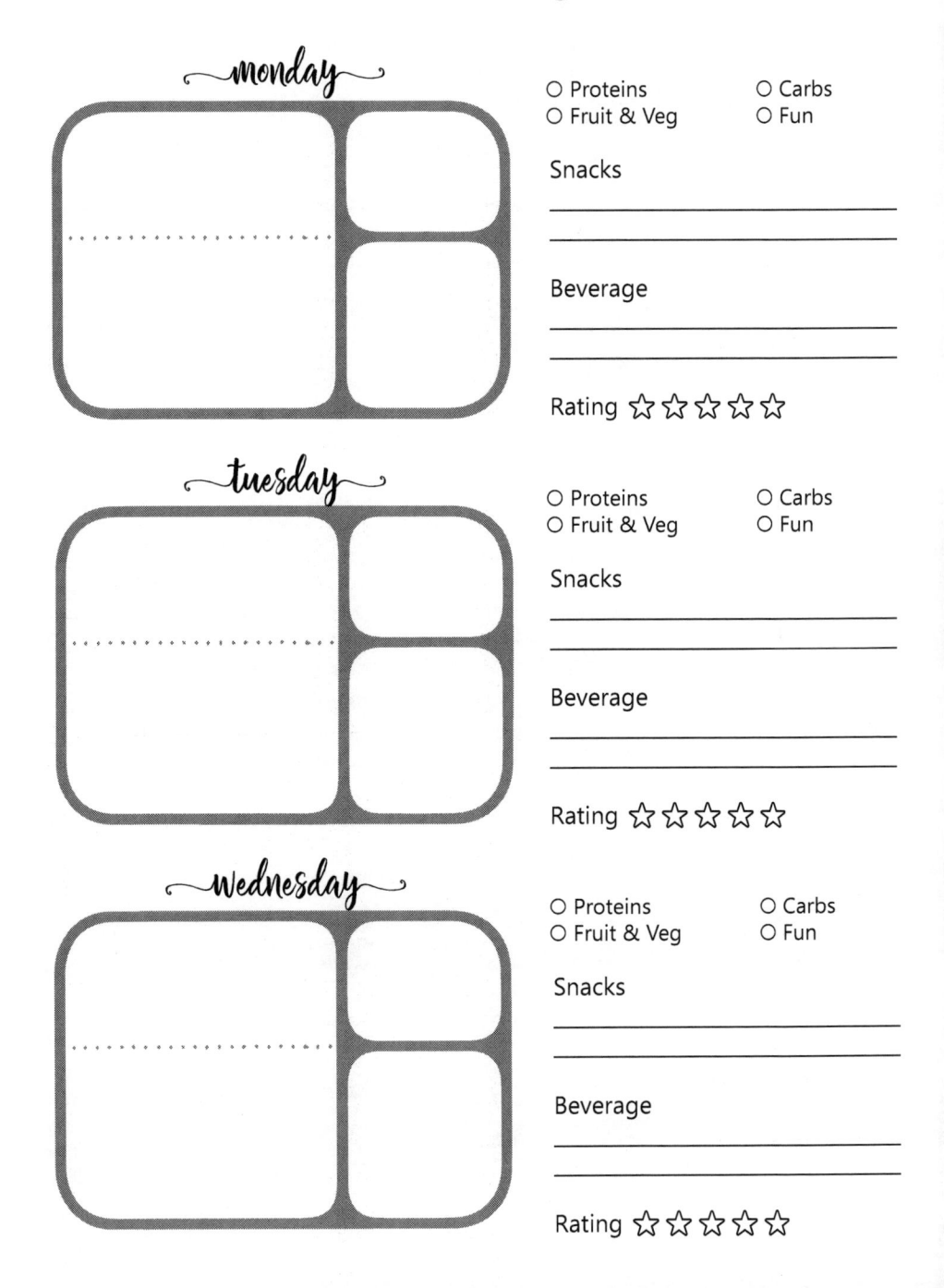

weekly

monday

○ Proteins ○ Carbs
○ Fruit & Veg ○ Fun

Snacks
_____
_____

Beverage
_____
_____

Rating ☆ ☆ ☆ ☆ ☆

tuesday

○ Proteins ○ Carbs
○ Fruit & Veg ○ Fun

Snacks
_____
_____

Beverage
_____
_____

Rating ☆ ☆ ☆ ☆ ☆

wednesday

○ Proteins ○ Carbs
○ Fruit & Veg ○ Fun

Snacks
_____
_____

Beverage
_____
_____

Rating ☆ ☆ ☆ ☆ ☆

lunch planner
FOR KIDS

thursday

○ Proteins ○ Carbs
○ Fruit & Veg ○ Fun

Snacks

Beverage

Rating ☆ ☆ ☆ ☆ ☆

friday

○ Proteins ○ Carbs
○ Fruit & Veg ○ Fun

Snacks

Beverage

Rating ☆ ☆ ☆ ☆ ☆

Favorites

Humm, please no more!

weekly

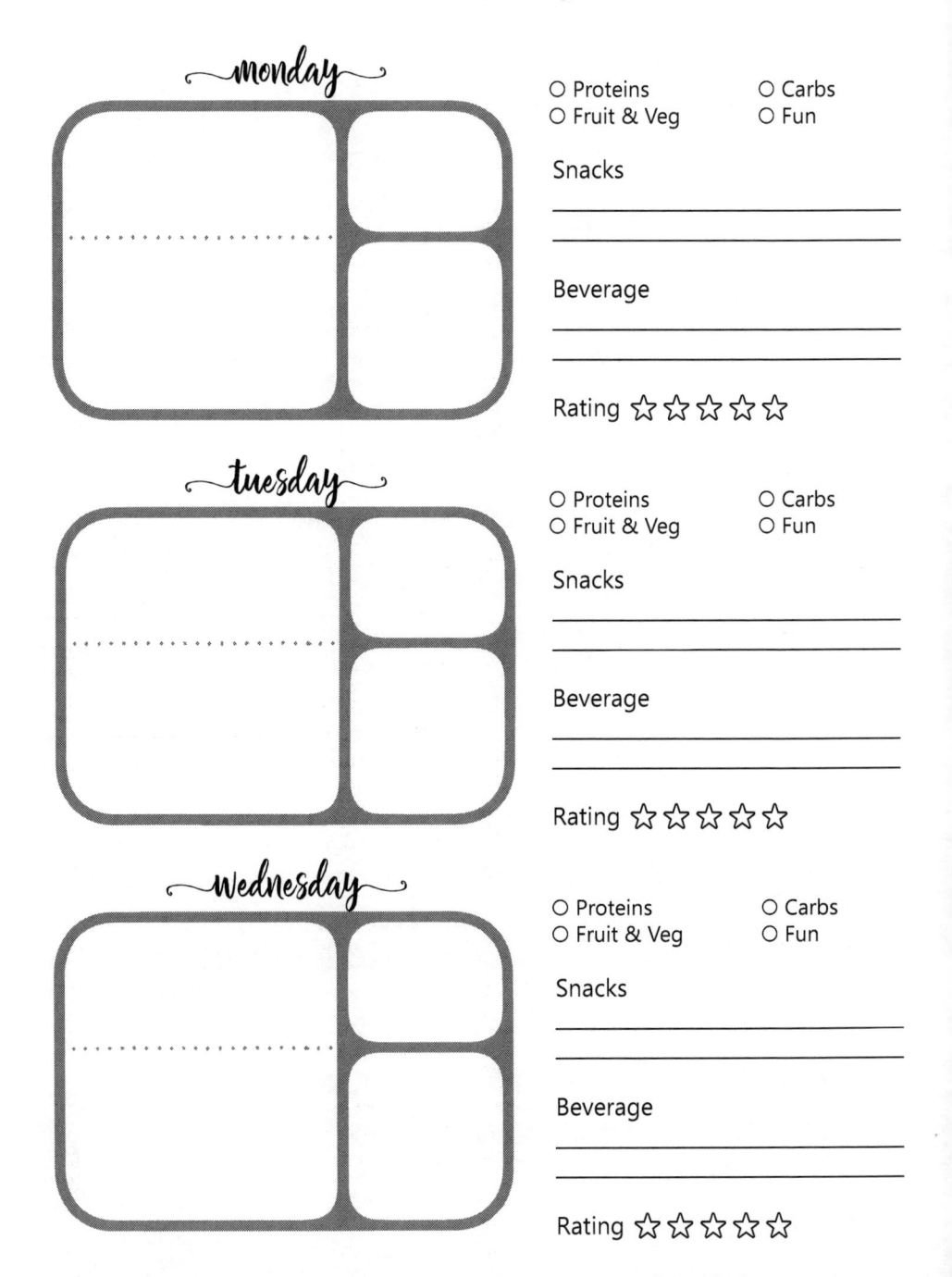

monday

○ Proteins ○ Carbs
○ Fruit & Veg ○ Fun

Snacks
_____
_____

Beverage
_____
_____

Rating ☆ ☆ ☆ ☆ ☆

tuesday

○ Proteins ○ Carbs
○ Fruit & Veg ○ Fun

Snacks
_____
_____

Beverage
_____
_____

Rating ☆ ☆ ☆ ☆ ☆

wednesday

○ Proteins ○ Carbs
○ Fruit & Veg ○ Fun

Snacks
_____
_____

Beverage
_____
_____

Rating ☆ ☆ ☆ ☆ ☆

lunch planner
FOR KIDS

thursday

○ Proteins ○ Carbs
○ Fruit & Veg ○ Fun

Snacks

Beverage

Rating ☆ ☆ ☆ ☆ ☆

friday

○ Proteins ○ Carbs
○ Fruit & Veg ○ Fun

Snacks

Beverage

Rating ☆ ☆ ☆ ☆ ☆

Favorites

Humm, please no more!

weekly

monday

○ Proteins   ○ Carbs
○ Fruit & Veg   ○ Fun

Snacks
_____
_____

Beverage
_____
_____

Rating ☆ ☆ ☆ ☆ ☆

tuesday

○ Proteins   ○ Carbs
○ Fruit & Veg   ○ Fun

Snacks
_____
_____

Beverage
_____
_____

Rating ☆ ☆ ☆ ☆ ☆

wednesday

○ Proteins   ○ Carbs
○ Fruit & Veg   ○ Fun

Snacks
_____
_____

Beverage
_____
_____

Rating ☆ ☆ ☆ ☆ ☆

lunch planner
FOR KIDS

thursday

○ Proteins ○ Carbs
○ Fruit & Veg ○ Fun

Snacks
_____
_____

Beverage
_____
_____

Rating ☆ ☆ ☆ ☆ ☆

friday

○ Proteins ○ Carbs
○ Fruit & Veg ○ Fun

Snacks
_____
_____

Beverage
_____
_____

Rating ☆ ☆ ☆ ☆ ☆

Favorites

Humm, please no more!

weekly

monday

○ Proteins ○ Carbs
○ Fruit & Veg ○ Fun

Snacks
_____
_____

Beverage
_____
_____

Rating ☆ ☆ ☆ ☆ ☆

tuesday

○ Proteins ○ Carbs
○ Fruit & Veg ○ Fun

Snacks
_____
_____

Beverage
_____
_____

Rating ☆ ☆ ☆ ☆ ☆

wednesday

○ Proteins ○ Carbs
○ Fruit & Veg ○ Fun

Snacks
_____
_____

Beverage
_____
_____

Rating ☆ ☆ ☆ ☆ ☆

lunch planner
FOR KIDS

thursday

○ Proteins ○ Carbs
○ Fruit & Veg ○ Fun

Snacks
___
___

Beverage
___
___

Rating ☆☆☆☆☆

friday

○ Proteins ○ Carbs
○ Fruit & Veg ○ Fun

Snacks
___
___

Beverage
___
___

Rating ☆☆☆☆☆

Favorites

Humm, please no more!

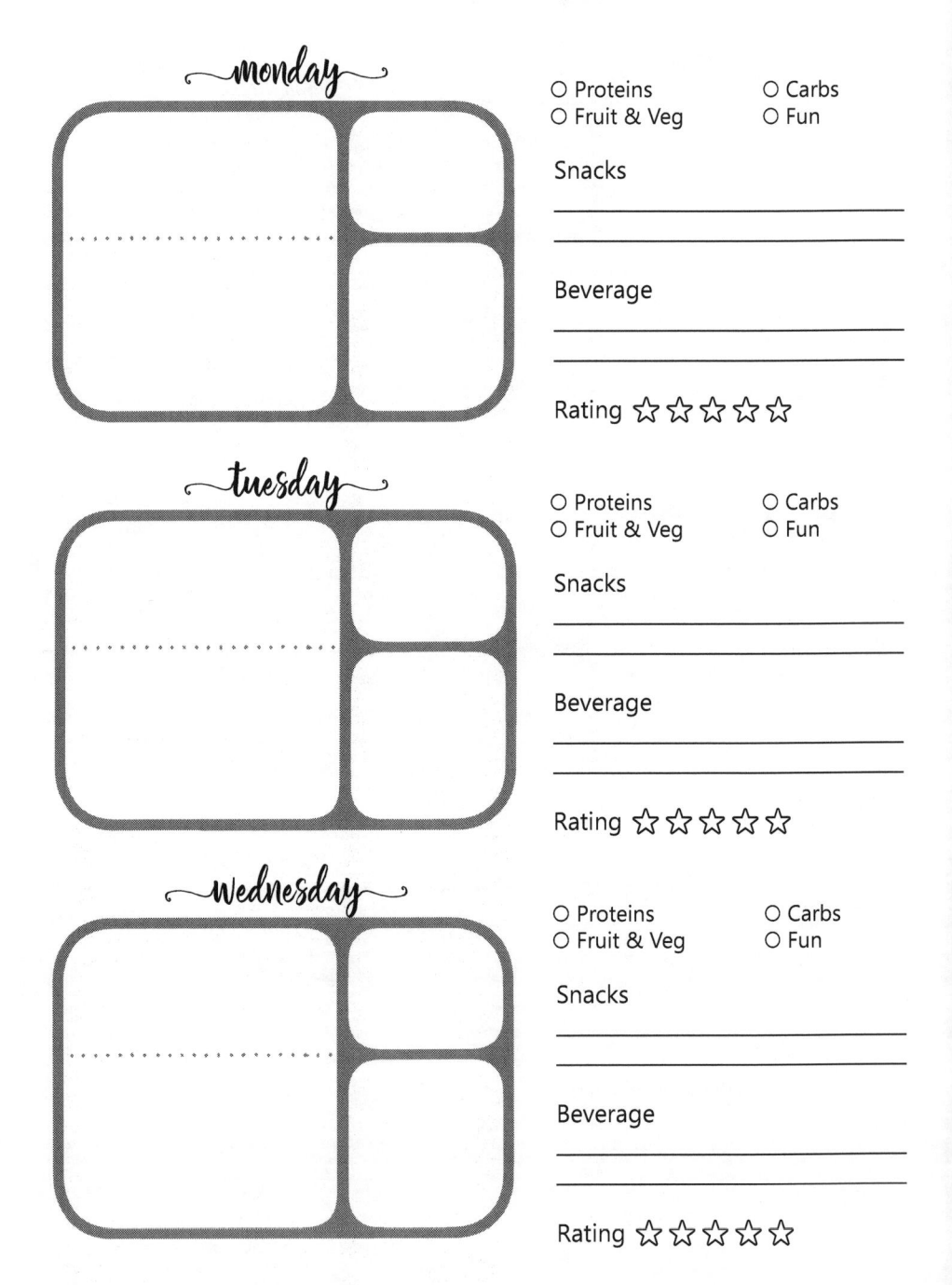

weekly

monday

○ Proteins   ○ Carbs
○ Fruit & Veg ○ Fun

Snacks
_____
_____

Beverage
_____
_____

Rating ☆ ☆ ☆ ☆ ☆

tuesday

○ Proteins   ○ Carbs
○ Fruit & Veg ○ Fun

Snacks
_____
_____

Beverage
_____
_____

Rating ☆ ☆ ☆ ☆ ☆

wednesday

○ Proteins   ○ Carbs
○ Fruit & Veg ○ Fun

Snacks
_____
_____

Beverage
_____
_____

Rating ☆ ☆ ☆ ☆ ☆

lunch planner
FOR KIDS

thursday

- ○ Proteins ○ Carbs
- ○ Fruit & Veg ○ Fun

Snacks

Beverage

Rating ☆ ☆ ☆ ☆ ☆

friday

- ○ Proteins ○ Carbs
- ○ Fruit & Veg ○ Fun

Snacks

Beverage

Rating ☆ ☆ ☆ ☆ ☆

Favorites

Humm, please no more!

weekly

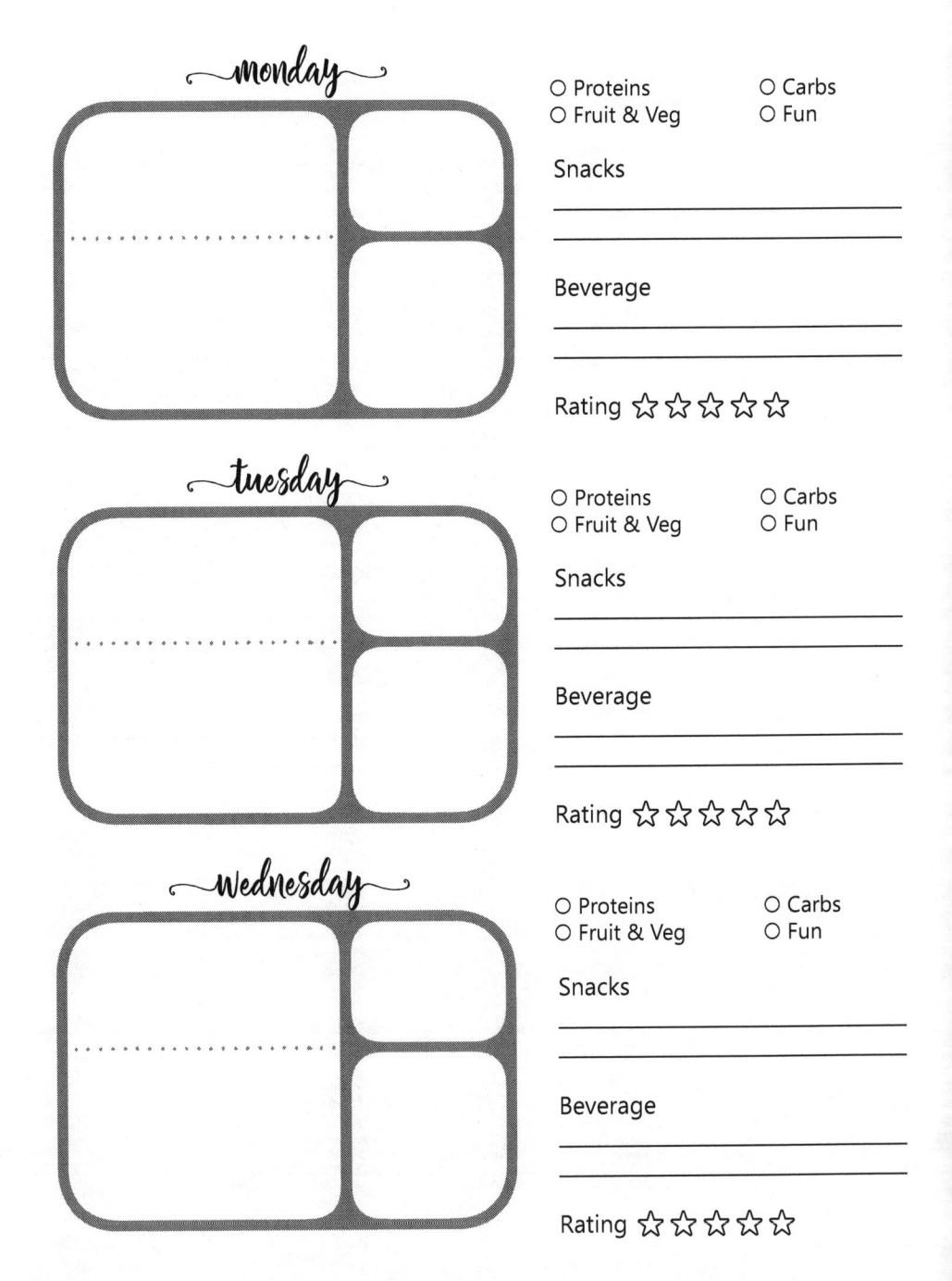

monday

○ Proteins   ○ Carbs
○ Fruit & Veg   ○ Fun

Snacks
_____
_____

Beverage
_____
_____

Rating ☆ ☆ ☆ ☆ ☆

tuesday

○ Proteins   ○ Carbs
○ Fruit & Veg   ○ Fun

Snacks
_____
_____

Beverage
_____
_____

Rating ☆ ☆ ☆ ☆ ☆

wednesday

○ Proteins   ○ Carbs
○ Fruit & Veg   ○ Fun

Snacks
_____
_____

Beverage
_____
_____

Rating ☆ ☆ ☆ ☆ ☆

lunch planner
FOR KIDS

thursday

- ○ Proteins   ○ Carbs
- ○ Fruit & Veg   ○ Fun

Snacks

Beverage

Rating ☆ ☆ ☆ ☆ ☆

friday

- ○ Proteins   ○ Carbs
- ○ Fruit & Veg   ○ Fun

Snacks

Beverage

Rating ☆ ☆ ☆ ☆ ☆

Favorites

Humm, please no more!

weekly

monday

○ Proteins ○ Carbs
○ Fruit & Veg ○ Fun

Snacks
_____
_____

Beverage
_____
_____

Rating ☆ ☆ ☆ ☆ ☆

tuesday

○ Proteins ○ Carbs
○ Fruit & Veg ○ Fun

Snacks
_____
_____

Beverage
_____
_____

Rating ☆ ☆ ☆ ☆ ☆

wednesday

○ Proteins ○ Carbs
○ Fruit & Veg ○ Fun

Snacks
_____
_____

Beverage
_____
_____

Rating ☆ ☆ ☆ ☆ ☆

lunch planner
FOR KIDS

thursday

○ Proteins ○ Carbs
○ Fruit & Veg ○ Fun

Snacks
_____
_____

Beverage
_____
_____

Rating ☆ ☆ ☆ ☆ ☆

friday

○ Proteins ○ Carbs
○ Fruit & Veg ○ Fun

Snacks
_____
_____

Beverage
_____
_____

Rating ☆ ☆ ☆ ☆ ☆

Favorites

Humm, please no more!

weekly

monday

○ Proteins ○ Carbs
○ Fruit & Veg ○ Fun

Snacks
_____
_____

Beverage
_____
_____

Rating ☆ ☆ ☆ ☆ ☆

tuesday

○ Proteins ○ Carbs
○ Fruit & Veg ○ Fun

Snacks
_____
_____

Beverage
_____
_____

Rating ☆ ☆ ☆ ☆ ☆

wednesday

○ Proteins ○ Carbs
○ Fruit & Veg ○ Fun

Snacks
_____
_____

Beverage
_____
_____

Rating ☆ ☆ ☆ ☆ ☆

lunch planner
FOR KIDS

thursday

○ Proteins ○ Carbs
○ Fruit & Veg ○ Fun

Snacks
_____
_____

Beverage
_____
_____

Rating ☆ ☆ ☆ ☆ ☆

friday

○ Proteins ○ Carbs
○ Fruit & Veg ○ Fun

Snacks
_____
_____

Beverage
_____
_____

Rating ☆ ☆ ☆ ☆ ☆

Favorites

Humm, please no more!

weekly

monday

○ Proteins　　○ Carbs
○ Fruit & Veg　○ Fun

Snacks
_____
_____

Beverage
_____
_____

Rating ☆☆☆☆☆

tuesday

○ Proteins　　○ Carbs
○ Fruit & Veg　○ Fun

Snacks
_____
_____

Beverage
_____
_____

Rating ☆☆☆☆☆

wednesday

○ Proteins　　○ Carbs
○ Fruit & Veg　○ Fun

Snacks
_____
_____

Beverage
_____
_____

Rating ☆☆☆☆☆

lunch planner
FOR KIDS

thursday

○ Proteins ○ Carbs
○ Fruit & Veg ○ Fun

Snacks
_____
_____

Beverage
_____
_____

Rating ☆ ☆ ☆ ☆ ☆

friday

○ Proteins ○ Carbs
○ Fruit & Veg ○ Fun

Snacks
_____
_____

Beverage
_____
_____

Rating ☆ ☆ ☆ ☆ ☆

Favorites

Humm, please no more!

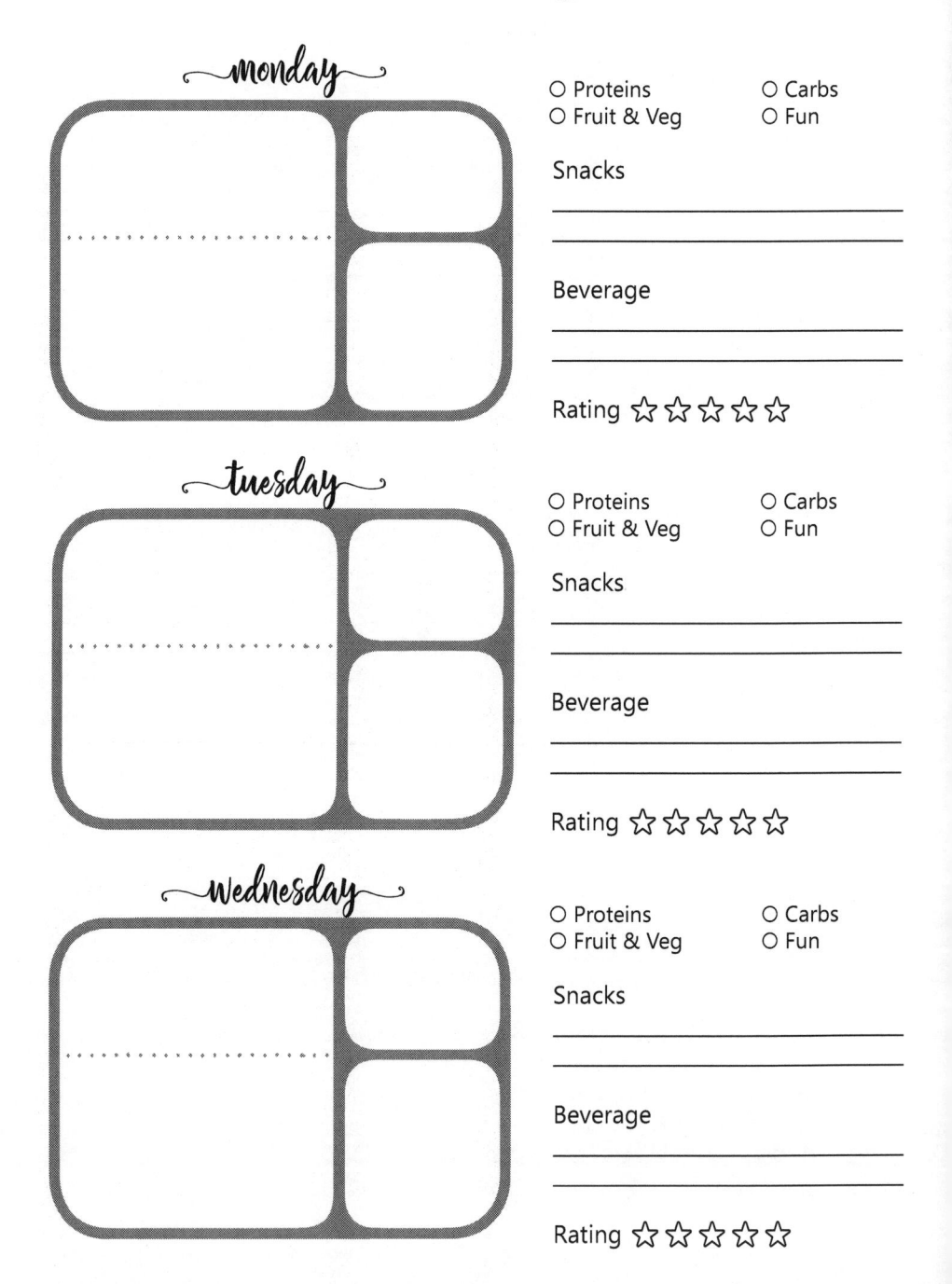

weekly

monday

- ○ Proteins　　○ Carbs
- ○ Fruit & Veg　○ Fun

Snacks
_____
_____

Beverage
_____
_____

Rating ☆ ☆ ☆ ☆ ☆

tuesday

- ○ Proteins　　○ Carbs
- ○ Fruit & Veg　○ Fun

Snacks
_____
_____

Beverage
_____
_____

Rating ☆ ☆ ☆ ☆ ☆

wednesday

- ○ Proteins　　○ Carbs
- ○ Fruit & Veg　○ Fun

Snacks
_____
_____

Beverage
_____
_____

Rating ☆ ☆ ☆ ☆ ☆

lunch planner
FOR KIDS

thursday

○ Proteins ○ Carbs
○ Fruit & Veg ○ Fun

Snacks
_____
_____

Beverage
_____
_____

Rating ☆ ☆ ☆ ☆ ☆

friday

○ Proteins ○ Carbs
○ Fruit & Veg ○ Fun

Snacks
_____
_____

Beverage
_____
_____

Rating ☆ ☆ ☆ ☆ ☆

Favorites

Humm, please no more!

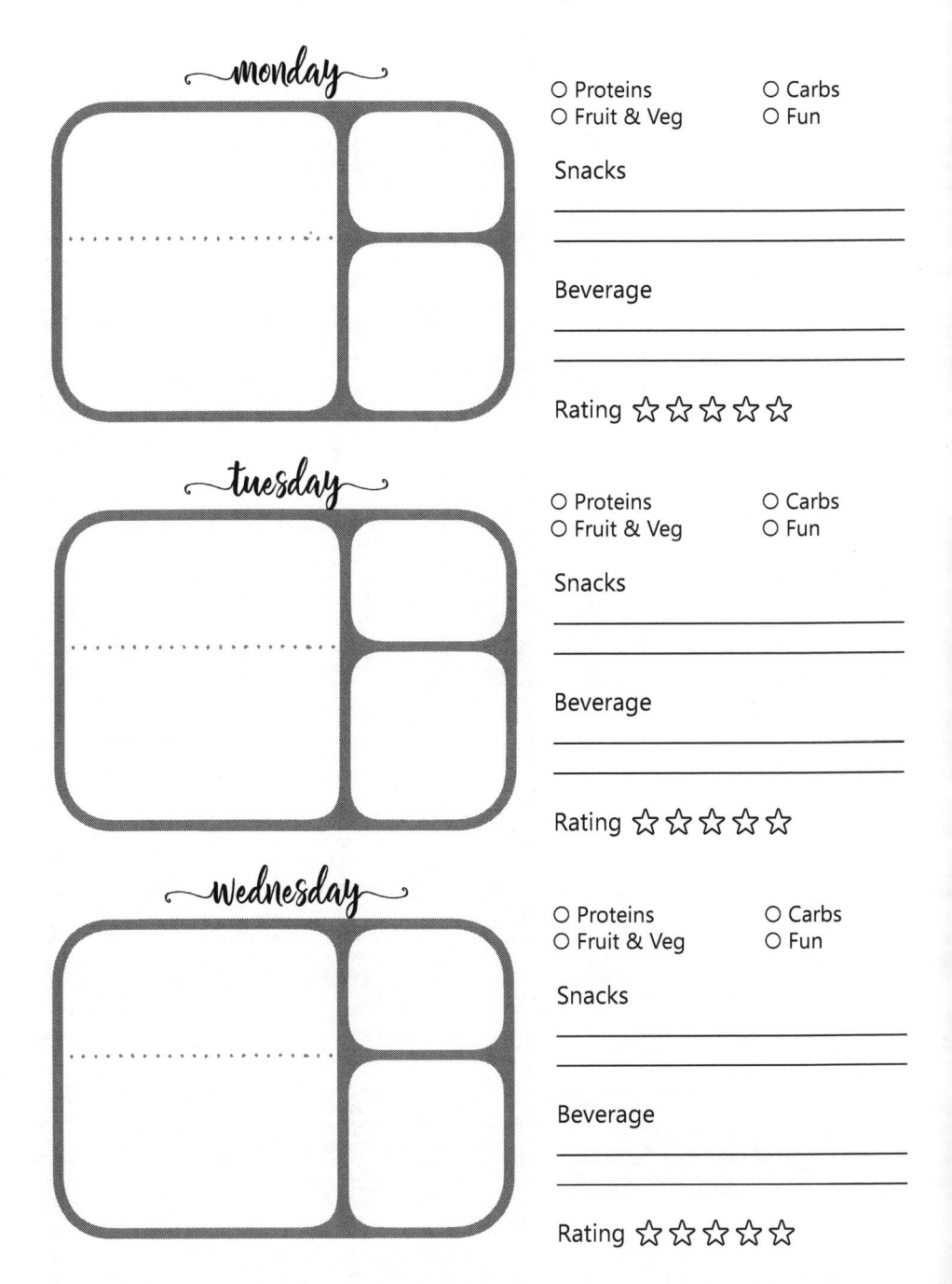

weekly

monday

○ Proteins   ○ Carbs
○ Fruit & Veg   ○ Fun

Snacks
_____
_____

Beverage
_____
_____

Rating ☆ ☆ ☆ ☆ ☆

tuesday

○ Proteins   ○ Carbs
○ Fruit & Veg   ○ Fun

Snacks
_____
_____

Beverage
_____
_____

Rating ☆ ☆ ☆ ☆ ☆

wednesday

○ Proteins   ○ Carbs
○ Fruit & Veg   ○ Fun

Snacks
_____
_____

Beverage
_____
_____

Rating ☆ ☆ ☆ ☆ ☆

lunch planner
FOR KIDS

thursday

○ Proteins   ○ Carbs
○ Fruit & Veg   ○ Fun

Snacks

Beverage

Rating ☆☆☆☆☆

friday

○ Proteins   ○ Carbs
○ Fruit & Veg   ○ Fun

Snacks

Beverage

Rating ☆☆☆☆☆

Favorites

Humm, please no more!

Weekly

monday

○ Proteins ○ Carbs
○ Fruit & Veg ○ Fun

Snacks

Beverage

Rating ☆☆☆☆☆

tuesday

○ Proteins ○ Carbs
○ Fruit & Veg ○ Fun

Snacks

Beverage

Rating ☆☆☆☆☆

wednesday

○ Proteins ○ Carbs
○ Fruit & Veg ○ Fun

Snacks

Beverage

Rating ☆☆☆☆☆

lunch planner
FOR KIDS

thursday

○ Proteins   ○ Carbs
○ Fruit & Veg   ○ Fun

Snacks

Beverage

Rating ☆ ☆ ☆ ☆ ☆

friday

○ Proteins   ○ Carbs
○ Fruit & Veg   ○ Fun

Snacks

Beverage

Rating ☆ ☆ ☆ ☆ ☆

Favorites

Humm, please no more!

weekly

monday

○ Proteins ○ Carbs
○ Fruit & Veg ○ Fun

Snacks

Beverage

Rating ☆☆☆☆☆

tuesday

○ Proteins ○ Carbs
○ Fruit & Veg ○ Fun

Snacks

Beverage

Rating ☆☆☆☆☆

wednesday

○ Proteins ○ Carbs
○ Fruit & Veg ○ Fun

Snacks

Beverage

Rating ☆☆☆☆☆

lunch planner
FOR KIDS

~thursday~

○ Proteins ○ Carbs
○ Fruit & Veg ○ Fun

Snacks
_____
_____

Beverage
_____
_____

Rating ☆ ☆ ☆ ☆ ☆

~friday~

○ Proteins ○ Carbs
○ Fruit & Veg ○ Fun

Snacks
_____
_____

Beverage
_____
_____

Rating ☆ ☆ ☆ ☆ ☆

Favorites

Humm, please no more!

weekly

monday

○ Proteins   ○ Carbs
○ Fruit & Veg   ○ Fun

Snacks

_____
_____

Beverage

_____

Rating ☆ ☆ ☆ ☆ ☆

tuesday

○ Proteins   ○ Carbs
○ Fruit & Veg   ○ Fun

Snacks

_____
_____

Beverage

_____

Rating ☆ ☆ ☆ ☆ ☆

wednesday

○ Proteins   ○ Carbs
○ Fruit & Veg   ○ Fun

Snacks

_____
_____

Beverage

_____

Rating ☆ ☆ ☆ ☆ ☆

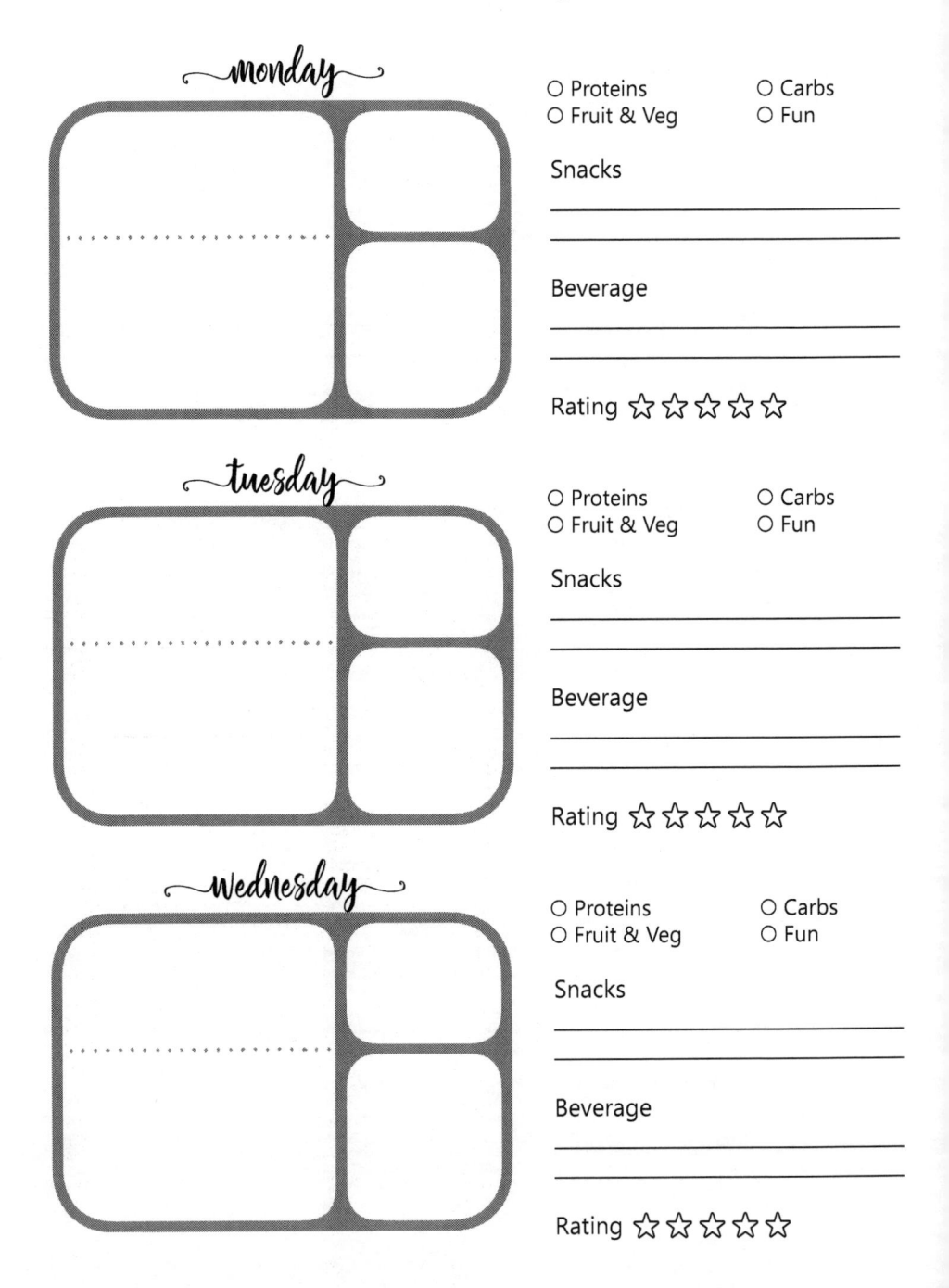

lunch planner
FOR KIDS

thursday

○ Proteins   ○ Carbs
○ Fruit & Veg   ○ Fun

Snacks
_____
_____

Beverage
_____
_____

Rating ☆ ☆ ☆ ☆ ☆

friday

○ Proteins   ○ Carbs
○ Fruit & Veg   ○ Fun

Snacks
_____
_____

Beverage
_____
_____

Rating ☆ ☆ ☆ ☆ ☆

Favorites

Humm, please no more!

weekly

monday

○ Proteins ○ Carbs
○ Fruit & Veg ○ Fun

Snacks
_____
_____

Beverage
_____
_____

Rating ☆ ☆ ☆ ☆ ☆

tuesday

○ Proteins ○ Carbs
○ Fruit & Veg ○ Fun

Snacks
_____
_____

Beverage
_____
_____

Rating ☆ ☆ ☆ ☆ ☆

wednesday

○ Proteins ○ Carbs
○ Fruit & Veg ○ Fun

Snacks
_____
_____

Beverage
_____
_____

Rating ☆ ☆ ☆ ☆ ☆

lunch planner
FOR KIDS

thursday

○ Proteins ○ Carbs
○ Fruit & Veg ○ Fun

Snacks

Beverage

Rating ☆ ☆ ☆ ☆ ☆

friday

○ Proteins ○ Carbs
○ Fruit & Veg ○ Fun

Snacks

Beverage

Rating ☆ ☆ ☆ ☆ ☆

Favorites

Humm, please no more!

weekly

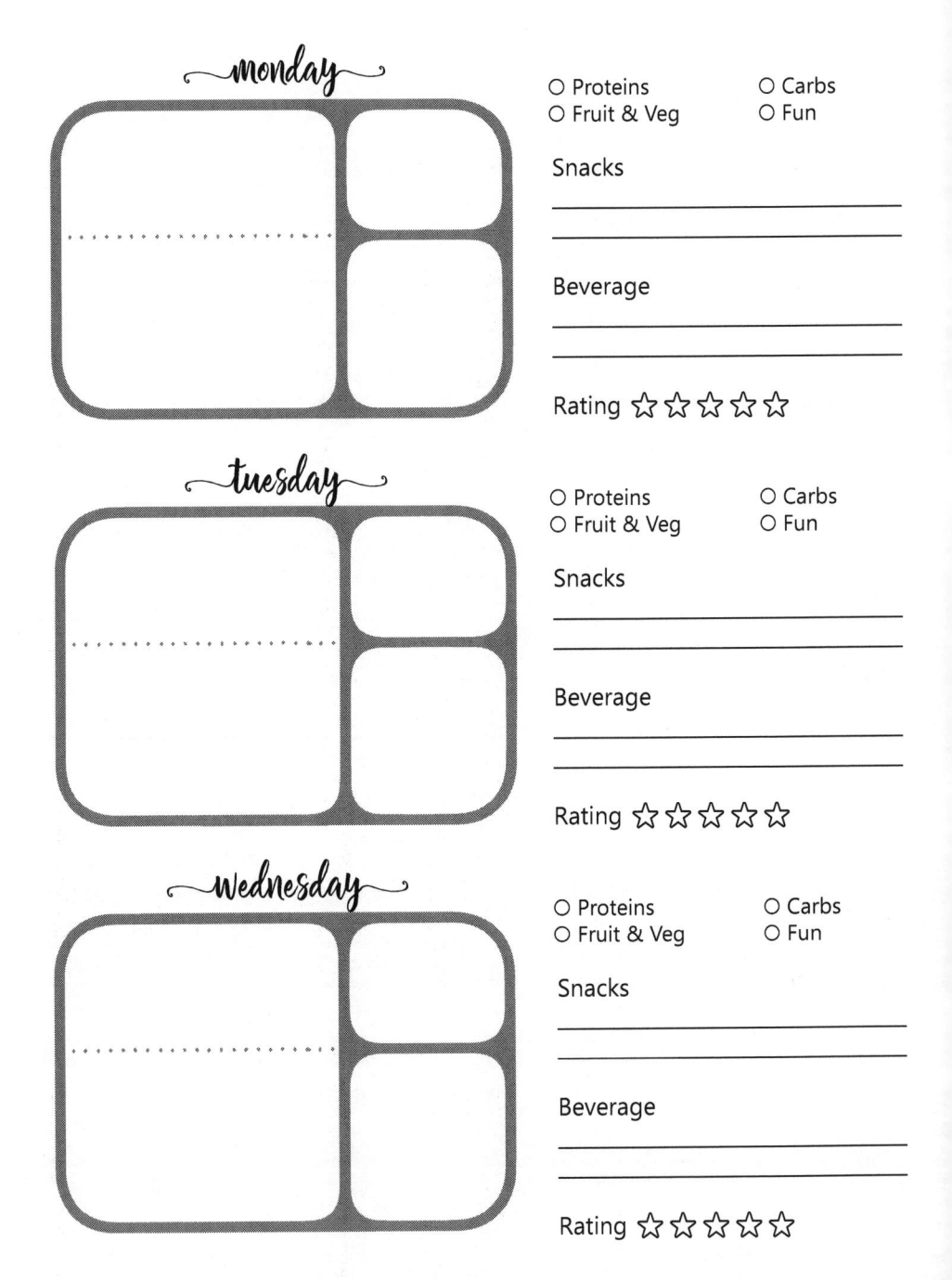

monday

○ Proteins   ○ Carbs
○ Fruit & Veg   ○ Fun

Snacks
_____
_____

Beverage
_____
_____

Rating ☆ ☆ ☆ ☆ ☆

tuesday

○ Proteins   ○ Carbs
○ Fruit & Veg   ○ Fun

Snacks
_____
_____

Beverage
_____
_____

Rating ☆ ☆ ☆ ☆ ☆

wednesday

○ Proteins   ○ Carbs
○ Fruit & Veg   ○ Fun

Snacks
_____
_____

Beverage
_____
_____

Rating ☆ ☆ ☆ ☆ ☆

lunch planner
FOR KIDS

thursday

- ○ Proteins
- ○ Fruit & Veg
- ○ Carbs
- ○ Fun

Snacks

Beverage

Rating ☆☆☆☆☆

friday

- ○ Proteins
- ○ Fruit & Veg
- ○ Carbs
- ○ Fun

Snacks

Beverage

Rating ☆☆☆☆☆

Favorites

Humm, please no more!

weekly

monday

○ Proteins   ○ Carbs
○ Fruit & Veg   ○ Fun

Snacks
_____
_____

Beverage
_____
_____

Rating ☆ ☆ ☆ ☆ ☆

tuesday

○ Proteins   ○ Carbs
○ Fruit & Veg   ○ Fun

Snacks
_____
_____

Beverage
_____
_____

Rating ☆ ☆ ☆ ☆ ☆

wednesday

○ Proteins   ○ Carbs
○ Fruit & Veg   ○ Fun

Snacks
_____
_____

Beverage
_____
_____

Rating ☆ ☆ ☆ ☆ ☆

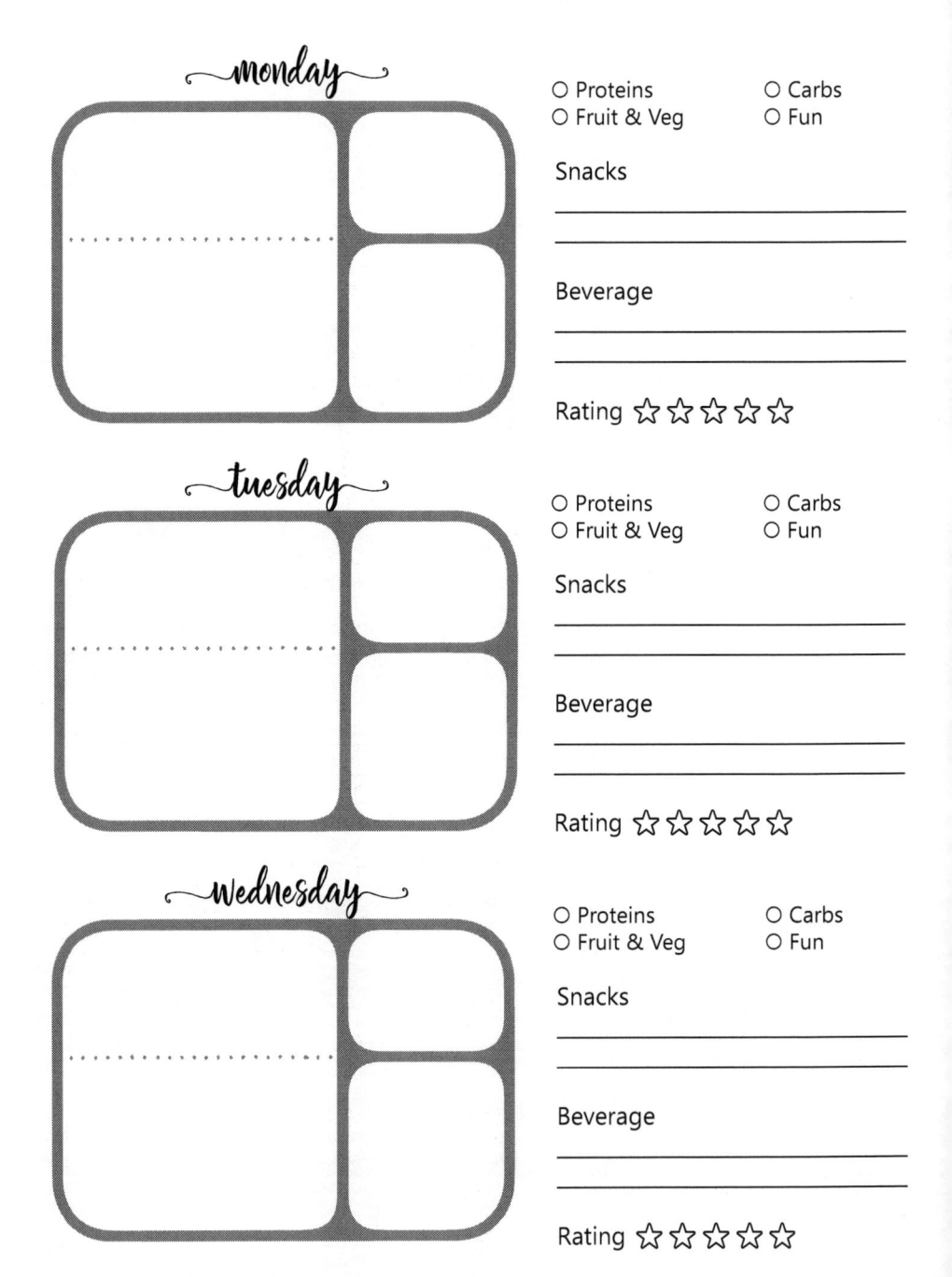

lunch planner
FOR KIDS

thursday

○ Proteins ○ Carbs
○ Fruit & Veg ○ Fun

Snacks

Beverage

Rating ☆ ☆ ☆ ☆ ☆

friday

○ Proteins ○ Carbs
○ Fruit & Veg ○ Fun

Snacks

Beverage

Rating ☆ ☆ ☆ ☆ ☆

Favorites

Humm, please no more!

weekly

monday

- ○ Proteins   ○ Carbs
- ○ Fruit & Veg   ○ Fun

Snacks

Beverage

Rating ☆☆☆☆☆

tuesday

- ○ Proteins   ○ Carbs
- ○ Fruit & Veg   ○ Fun

Snacks

Beverage

Rating ☆☆☆☆☆

wednesday

- ○ Proteins   ○ Carbs
- ○ Fruit & Veg   ○ Fun

Snacks

Beverage

Rating ☆☆☆☆☆

lunch planner
FOR KIDS

thursday

○ Proteins ○ Carbs
○ Fruit & Veg ○ Fun

Snacks

Beverage

Rating ☆ ☆ ☆ ☆ ☆

friday

○ Proteins ○ Carbs
○ Fruit & Veg ○ Fun

Snacks

Beverage

Rating ☆ ☆ ☆ ☆ ☆

Favorites

Humm, please no more!

weekly

monday

○ Proteins ○ Carbs
○ Fruit & Veg ○ Fun

Snacks

Beverage

Rating ☆☆☆☆☆

tuesday

○ Proteins ○ Carbs
○ Fruit & Veg ○ Fun

Snacks

Beverage

Rating ☆☆☆☆☆

wednesday

○ Proteins ○ Carbs
○ Fruit & Veg ○ Fun

Snacks

Beverage

Rating ☆☆☆☆☆

lunch planner
FOR KIDS

thursday

○ Proteins   ○ Carbs
○ Fruit & Veg   ○ Fun

Snacks

Beverage

Rating ☆ ☆ ☆ ☆ ☆

friday

○ Proteins   ○ Carbs
○ Fruit & Veg   ○ Fun

Snacks

Beverage

Rating ☆ ☆ ☆ ☆ ☆

Favorites

Humm, please no more!

weekly

monday

○ Proteins ○ Carbs
○ Fruit & Veg ○ Fun

Snacks
_____
_____

Beverage
_____
_____

Rating ☆ ☆ ☆ ☆ ☆

tuesday

○ Proteins ○ Carbs
○ Fruit & Veg ○ Fun

Snacks
_____
_____

Beverage
_____
_____

Rating ☆ ☆ ☆ ☆ ☆

wednesday

○ Proteins ○ Carbs
○ Fruit & Veg ○ Fun

Snacks
_____
_____

Beverage
_____
_____

Rating ☆ ☆ ☆ ☆ ☆

lunch planner
FOR KIDS

thursday

○ Proteins ○ Carbs
○ Fruit & Veg ○ Fun

Snacks

Beverage

Rating ☆ ☆ ☆ ☆ ☆

friday

○ Proteins ○ Carbs
○ Fruit & Veg ○ Fun

Snacks

Beverage

Rating ☆ ☆ ☆ ☆ ☆

Favorites

Humm, please no more!

weekly

monday

○ Proteins   ○ Carbs
○ Fruit & Veg   ○ Fun

Snacks

Beverage

Rating ☆ ☆ ☆ ☆ ☆

tuesday

○ Proteins   ○ Carbs
○ Fruit & Veg   ○ Fun

Snacks

Beverage

Rating ☆ ☆ ☆ ☆ ☆

wednesday

○ Proteins   ○ Carbs
○ Fruit & Veg   ○ Fun

Snacks

Beverage

Rating ☆ ☆ ☆ ☆ ☆

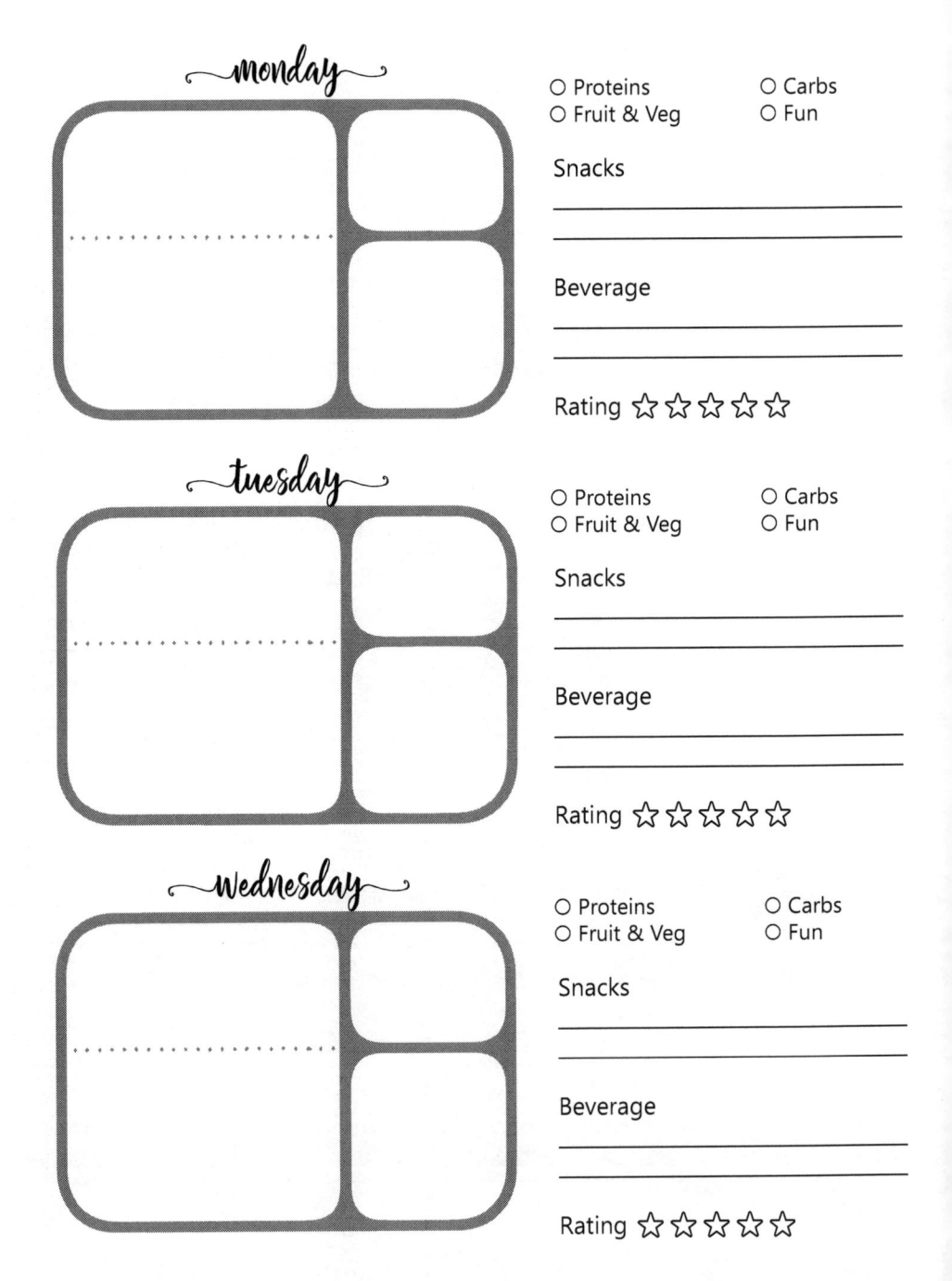

lunch planner
FOR KIDS

thursday

○ Proteins   ○ Carbs
○ Fruit & Veg   ○ Fun

Snacks
_____
_____

Beverage
_____
_____

Rating ☆ ☆ ☆ ☆ ☆

friday

○ Proteins   ○ Carbs
○ Fruit & Veg   ○ Fun

Snacks
_____
_____

Beverage
_____
_____

Rating ☆ ☆ ☆ ☆ ☆

Favorites

Humm, please no more!

weekly

monday

○ Proteins ○ Carbs
○ Fruit & Veg ○ Fun

Snacks
_____
_____

Beverage
_____
_____

Rating ☆ ☆ ☆ ☆ ☆

tuesday

○ Proteins ○ Carbs
○ Fruit & Veg ○ Fun

Snacks
_____
_____

Beverage
_____
_____

Rating ☆ ☆ ☆ ☆ ☆

wednesday

○ Proteins ○ Carbs
○ Fruit & Veg ○ Fun

Snacks
_____
_____

Beverage
_____
_____

Rating ☆ ☆ ☆ ☆ ☆

lunch planner
FOR KIDS

thursday

○ Proteins   ○ Carbs
○ Fruit & Veg   ○ Fun

Snacks

Beverage

Rating ☆ ☆ ☆ ☆ ☆

friday

○ Proteins   ○ Carbs
○ Fruit & Veg   ○ Fun

Snacks

Beverage

Rating ☆ ☆ ☆ ☆ ☆

Favorites

Humm, please no more!

weekly

monday

○ Proteins   ○ Carbs
○ Fruit & Veg   ○ Fun

Snacks
_____
_____

Beverage
_____
_____

Rating ☆☆☆☆☆

tuesday

○ Proteins   ○ Carbs
○ Fruit & Veg   ○ Fun

Snacks
_____
_____

Beverage
_____
_____

Rating ☆☆☆☆☆

wednesday

○ Proteins   ○ Carbs
○ Fruit & Veg   ○ Fun

Snacks
_____
_____

Beverage
_____
_____

Rating ☆☆☆☆☆

lunch planner
FOR KIDS

thursday

○ Proteins ○ Carbs
○ Fruit & Veg ○ Fun

Snacks
_____
_____

Beverage
_____
_____

Rating ☆ ☆ ☆ ☆ ☆

friday

○ Proteins ○ Carbs
○ Fruit & Veg ○ Fun

Snacks
_____
_____

Beverage
_____
_____

Rating ☆ ☆ ☆ ☆ ☆

Favorites

Humm, please no more!

Weekly

monday

○ Proteins   ○ Carbs
○ Fruit & Veg   ○ Fun

Snacks
_____
_____

Beverage
_____
_____

Rating ☆ ☆ ☆ ☆ ☆

tuesday

○ Proteins   ○ Carbs
○ Fruit & Veg   ○ Fun

Snacks
_____
_____

Beverage
_____
_____

Rating ☆ ☆ ☆ ☆ ☆

wednesday

○ Proteins   ○ Carbs
○ Fruit & Veg   ○ Fun

Snacks
_____
_____

Beverage
_____
_____

Rating ☆ ☆ ☆ ☆ ☆

lunch planner
FOR KIDS

thursday

○ Proteins ○ Carbs
○ Fruit & Veg ○ Fun

Snacks
_____
_____

Beverage
_____
_____

Rating ☆ ☆ ☆ ☆ ☆

friday

○ Proteins ○ Carbs
○ Fruit & Veg ○ Fun

Snacks
_____
_____

Beverage
_____
_____

Rating ☆ ☆ ☆ ☆ ☆

Favorites

Humm, please no more!

Weekly

monday

○ Proteins ○ Carbs
○ Fruit & Veg ○ Fun

Snacks
_____
_____

Beverage
_____
_____

Rating ☆☆☆☆☆

tuesday

○ Proteins ○ Carbs
○ Fruit & Veg ○ Fun

Snacks
_____
_____

Beverage
_____
_____

Rating ☆☆☆☆☆

wednesday

○ Proteins ○ Carbs
○ Fruit & Veg ○ Fun

Snacks
_____
_____

Beverage
_____
_____

Rating ☆☆☆☆☆

lunch planner
FOR KIDS

thursday

○ Proteins   ○ Carbs
○ Fruit & Veg   ○ Fun

Snacks

Beverage

Rating ☆☆☆☆☆

friday

○ Proteins   ○ Carbs
○ Fruit & Veg   ○ Fun

Snacks

Beverage

Rating ☆☆☆☆☆

Favorites

Humm, please no more!

Weekly

monday

○ Proteins   ○ Carbs
○ Fruit & Veg   ○ Fun

Snacks
_____
_____

Beverage
_____
_____

Rating ☆ ☆ ☆ ☆ ☆

tuesday

○ Proteins   ○ Carbs
○ Fruit & Veg   ○ Fun

Snacks
_____
_____

Beverage
_____
_____

Rating ☆ ☆ ☆ ☆ ☆

wednesday

○ Proteins   ○ Carbs
○ Fruit & Veg   ○ Fun

Snacks
_____
_____

Beverage
_____
_____

Rating ☆ ☆ ☆ ☆ ☆

lunch planner
FOR KIDS

thursday

○ Proteins　　○ Carbs
○ Fruit & Veg　○ Fun

Snacks

Beverage

Rating ☆☆☆☆☆

friday

○ Proteins　　○ Carbs
○ Fruit & Veg　○ Fun

Snacks

Beverage

Rating ☆☆☆☆☆

Favorites

Humm, please no more!

Weekly

monday

○ Proteins ○ Carbs
○ Fruit & Veg ○ Fun

Snacks

Beverage

Rating ☆☆☆☆☆

tuesday

○ Proteins ○ Carbs
○ Fruit & Veg ○ Fun

Snacks

Beverage

Rating ☆☆☆☆☆

wednesday

○ Proteins ○ Carbs
○ Fruit & Veg ○ Fun

Snacks

Beverage

Rating ☆☆☆☆☆

lunch planner
FOR KIDS

thursday

○ Proteins   ○ Carbs
○ Fruit & Veg   ○ Fun

Snacks

Beverage

Rating ☆ ☆ ☆ ☆ ☆

friday

○ Proteins   ○ Carbs
○ Fruit & Veg   ○ Fun

Snacks

Beverage

Rating ☆ ☆ ☆ ☆ ☆

Favorites

Humm, please no more!

Weekly

monday

○ Proteins ○ Carbs
○ Fruit & Veg ○ Fun

Snacks

Beverage

Rating ☆☆☆☆☆

tuesday

○ Proteins ○ Carbs
○ Fruit & Veg ○ Fun

Snacks

Beverage

Rating ☆☆☆☆☆

wednesday

○ Proteins ○ Carbs
○ Fruit & Veg ○ Fun

Snacks

Beverage

Rating ☆☆☆☆☆

lunch planner
FOR KIDS

thursday

○ Proteins ○ Carbs
○ Fruit & Veg ○ Fun

Snacks

Beverage

Rating ☆ ☆ ☆ ☆ ☆

friday

○ Proteins ○ Carbs
○ Fruit & Veg ○ Fun

Snacks

Beverage

Rating ☆ ☆ ☆ ☆ ☆

Favorites

Humm, please no more!

Weekly

monday

○ Proteins ○ Carbs
○ Fruit & Veg ○ Fun

Snacks
_____
_____

Beverage
_____
_____

Rating ☆ ☆ ☆ ☆ ☆

tuesday

○ Proteins ○ Carbs
○ Fruit & Veg ○ Fun

Snacks
_____
_____

Beverage
_____
_____

Rating ☆ ☆ ☆ ☆ ☆

wednesday

○ Proteins ○ Carbs
○ Fruit & Veg ○ Fun

Snacks
_____
_____

Beverage
_____
_____

Rating ☆ ☆ ☆ ☆ ☆

lunch planner
FOR KIDS

thursday

○ Proteins ○ Carbs
○ Fruit & Veg ○ Fun

Snacks

Beverage

Rating ☆☆☆☆☆

friday

○ Proteins ○ Carbs
○ Fruit & Veg ○ Fun

Snacks

Beverage

Rating ☆☆☆☆☆

Favorites

Humm, please no more!

Weekly

monday

○ Proteins ○ Carbs
○ Fruit & Veg ○ Fun

Snacks
_____
_____

Beverage
_____
_____

Rating ☆☆☆☆☆

tuesday

○ Proteins ○ Carbs
○ Fruit & Veg ○ Fun

Snacks
_____
_____

Beverage
_____
_____

Rating ☆☆☆☆☆

wednesday

○ Proteins ○ Carbs
○ Fruit & Veg ○ Fun

Snacks
_____
_____

Beverage
_____
_____

Rating ☆☆☆☆☆

lunch planner
FOR KIDS

thursday

○ Proteins ○ Carbs
○ Fruit & Veg ○ Fun

Snacks
_____
_____

Beverage
_____
_____

Rating ☆ ☆ ☆ ☆ ☆

friday

○ Proteins ○ Carbs
○ Fruit & Veg ○ Fun

Snacks
_____
_____

Beverage
_____
_____

Rating ☆ ☆ ☆ ☆ ☆

Favorites

Humm, please no more!

Weekly

monday

○ Proteins ○ Carbs
○ Fruit & Veg ○ Fun

Snacks

Beverage

Rating ☆☆☆☆☆

tuesday

○ Proteins ○ Carbs
○ Fruit & Veg ○ Fun

Snacks

Beverage

Rating ☆☆☆☆☆

wednesday

○ Proteins ○ Carbs
○ Fruit & Veg ○ Fun

Snacks

Beverage

Rating ☆☆☆☆☆

lunch planner
FOR KIDS

thursday

○ Proteins ○ Carbs
○ Fruit & Veg ○ Fun

Snacks

Beverage

Rating ☆ ☆ ☆ ☆ ☆

friday

○ Proteins ○ Carbs
○ Fruit & Veg ○ Fun

Snacks

Beverage

Rating ☆ ☆ ☆ ☆ ☆

Favorites

Humm, please no more!

Weekly

monday

- ○ Proteins
- ○ Fruit & Veg
- ○ Carbs
- ○ Fun

Snacks

Beverage

Rating ☆☆☆☆☆

tuesday

- ○ Proteins
- ○ Fruit & Veg
- ○ Carbs
- ○ Fun

Snacks

Beverage

Rating ☆☆☆☆☆

wednesday

- ○ Proteins
- ○ Fruit & Veg
- ○ Carbs
- ○ Fun

Snacks

Beverage

Rating ☆☆☆☆☆

lunch planner
FOR KIDS

thursday

○ Proteins ○ Carbs
○ Fruit & Veg ○ Fun

Snacks

Beverage

Rating ☆ ☆ ☆ ☆ ☆

friday

○ Proteins ○ Carbs
○ Fruit & Veg ○ Fun

Snacks

Beverage

Rating ☆ ☆ ☆ ☆ ☆

Favorites

Humm, please no more!

Weekly

monday

○ Proteins   ○ Carbs
○ Fruit & Veg   ○ Fun

Snacks

Beverage

Rating ☆☆☆☆☆

tuesday

○ Proteins   ○ Carbs
○ Fruit & Veg   ○ Fun

Snacks

Beverage

Rating ☆☆☆☆☆

wednesday

○ Proteins   ○ Carbs
○ Fruit & Veg   ○ Fun

Snacks

Beverage

Rating ☆☆☆☆☆

lunch planner
FOR KIDS

thursday

○ Proteins ○ Carbs
○ Fruit & Veg ○ Fun

Snacks

Beverage

Rating ☆☆☆☆☆

friday

○ Proteins ○ Carbs
○ Fruit & Veg ○ Fun

Snacks

Beverage

Rating ☆☆☆☆☆

Favorites

Humm, please no more!

Weekly

monday

○ Proteins ○ Carbs
○ Fruit & Veg ○ Fun

Snacks
_____
_____

Beverage
_____
_____

Rating ☆☆☆☆☆

tuesday

○ Proteins ○ Carbs
○ Fruit & Veg ○ Fun

Snacks
_____
_____

Beverage
_____
_____

Rating ☆☆☆☆☆

wednesday

○ Proteins ○ Carbs
○ Fruit & Veg ○ Fun

Snacks
_____
_____

Beverage
_____
_____

Rating ☆☆☆☆☆

lunch planner
FOR KIDS

thursday

○ Proteins   ○ Carbs
○ Fruit & Veg   ○ Fun

Snacks

Beverage

Rating ☆☆☆☆☆

friday

○ Proteins   ○ Carbs
○ Fruit & Veg   ○ Fun

Snacks

Beverage

Rating ☆☆☆☆☆

Favorites

Humm, please no more!

Weekly

monday

○ Proteins ○ Carbs
○ Fruit & Veg ○ Fun

Snacks

Beverage

Rating ☆☆☆☆☆

tuesday

○ Proteins ○ Carbs
○ Fruit & Veg ○ Fun

Snacks

Beverage

Rating ☆☆☆☆☆

wednesday

○ Proteins ○ Carbs
○ Fruit & Veg ○ Fun

Snacks

Beverage

Rating ☆☆☆☆☆

lunch planner
FOR KIDS

thursday

○ Proteins   ○ Carbs
○ Fruit & Veg   ○ Fun

Snacks

Beverage

Rating ☆ ☆ ☆ ☆ ☆

friday

○ Proteins   ○ Carbs
○ Fruit & Veg   ○ Fun

Snacks

Beverage

Rating ☆ ☆ ☆ ☆ ☆

Favorites

Humm, please no more!

weekly

monday

- ○ Proteins
- ○ Fruit & Veg
- ○ Carbs
- ○ Fun

Snacks
_____
_____

Beverage
_____

Rating ☆ ☆ ☆ ☆ ☆

tuesday

- ○ Proteins
- ○ Fruit & Veg
- ○ Carbs
- ○ Fun

Snacks
_____
_____

Beverage
_____

Rating ☆ ☆ ☆ ☆ ☆

wednesday

- ○ Proteins
- ○ Fruit & Veg
- ○ Carbs
- ○ Fun

Snacks
_____
_____

Beverage
_____

Rating ☆ ☆ ☆ ☆ ☆

lunch planner
FOR KIDS

thursday

○ Proteins   ○ Carbs
○ Fruit & Veg ○ Fun

Snacks

Beverage

Rating ☆☆☆☆☆

friday

○ Proteins   ○ Carbs
○ Fruit & Veg ○ Fun

Snacks

Beverage

Rating ☆☆☆☆☆

Favorites

Humm, please no more!

Weekly

monday

○ Proteins ○ Carbs
○ Fruit & Veg ○ Fun

Snacks
_____
_____

Beverage
_____
_____

Rating ☆☆☆☆☆

tuesday

○ Proteins ○ Carbs
○ Fruit & Veg ○ Fun

Snacks
_____
_____

Beverage
_____
_____

Rating ☆☆☆☆☆

wednesday

○ Proteins ○ Carbs
○ Fruit & Veg ○ Fun

Snacks
_____
_____

Beverage
_____
_____

Rating ☆☆☆☆☆

lunch planner
FOR KIDS

thursday

○ Proteins ○ Carbs
○ Fruit & Veg ○ Fun

Snacks

Beverage

Rating ☆☆☆☆☆

friday

○ Proteins ○ Carbs
○ Fruit & Veg ○ Fun

Snacks

Beverage

Rating ☆☆☆☆☆

Favorites

Humm, please no more!

Weekly

monday

○ Proteins ○ Carbs
○ Fruit & Veg ○ Fun

Snacks

Beverage

Rating ☆☆☆☆☆

tuesday

○ Proteins ○ Carbs
○ Fruit & Veg ○ Fun

Snacks

Beverage

Rating ☆☆☆☆☆

wednesday

○ Proteins ○ Carbs
○ Fruit & Veg ○ Fun

Snacks

Beverage

Rating ☆☆☆☆☆

lunch planner
FOR KIDS

thursday

○ Proteins   ○ Carbs
○ Fruit & Veg   ○ Fun

Snacks

Beverage

Rating ☆☆☆☆☆

friday

○ Proteins   ○ Carbs
○ Fruit & Veg   ○ Fun

Snacks

Beverage

Rating ☆☆☆☆☆

Favorites

Humm, please no more!

Weekly

monday

○ Proteins   ○ Carbs
○ Fruit & Veg   ○ Fun

Snacks

Beverage

Rating ☆☆☆☆☆

tuesday

○ Proteins   ○ Carbs
○ Fruit & Veg   ○ Fun

Snacks

Beverage

Rating ☆☆☆☆☆

wednesday

○ Proteins   ○ Carbs
○ Fruit & Veg   ○ Fun

Snacks

Beverage

Rating ☆☆☆☆☆

lunch planner
FOR KIDS

thursday

○ Proteins　　○ Carbs
○ Fruit & Veg　○ Fun

Snacks

Beverage

Rating ☆☆☆☆☆

friday

○ Proteins　　○ Carbs
○ Fruit & Veg　○ Fun

Snacks

Beverage

Rating ☆☆☆☆☆

Favorites

Humm, please no more!

Weekly

monday

○ Proteins   ○ Carbs
○ Fruit & Veg   ○ Fun

Snacks

_____
_____

Beverage

_____
_____

Rating ☆☆☆☆☆

tuesday

○ Proteins   ○ Carbs
○ Fruit & Veg   ○ Fun

Snacks

_____
_____

Beverage

_____
_____

Rating ☆☆☆☆☆

wednesday

○ Proteins   ○ Carbs
○ Fruit & Veg   ○ Fun

Snacks

_____
_____

Beverage

_____
_____

Rating ☆☆☆☆☆

lunch planner
FOR KIDS

thursday

○ Proteins ○ Carbs
○ Fruit & Veg ○ Fun

Snacks

Beverage

Rating ☆☆☆☆☆

friday

○ Proteins ○ Carbs
○ Fruit & Veg ○ Fun

Snacks

Beverage

Rating ☆☆☆☆☆

Favorites

Humm, please no more!

Weekly

monday

○ Proteins ○ Carbs
○ Fruit & Veg ○ Fun

Snacks

Beverage

Rating ☆☆☆☆☆

tuesday

○ Proteins ○ Carbs
○ Fruit & Veg ○ Fun

Snacks

Beverage

Rating ☆☆☆☆☆

wednesday

○ Proteins ○ Carbs
○ Fruit & Veg ○ Fun

Snacks

Beverage

Rating ☆☆☆☆☆

lunch planner
FOR KIDS

thursday

○ Proteins   ○ Carbs
○ Fruit & Veg   ○ Fun

Snacks
_____
_____

Beverage
_____
_____

Rating ☆☆☆☆☆

friday

○ Proteins   ○ Carbs
○ Fruit & Veg   ○ Fun

Snacks
_____
_____

Beverage
_____
_____

Rating ☆☆☆☆☆

Favorites

Humm, please no more!

Weekly

monday

○ Proteins ○ Carbs
○ Fruit & Veg ○ Fun

Snacks
_____
_____

Beverage
_____
_____

Rating ☆ ☆ ☆ ☆ ☆

tuesday

○ Proteins ○ Carbs
○ Fruit & Veg ○ Fun

Snacks
_____
_____

Beverage
_____
_____

Rating ☆ ☆ ☆ ☆ ☆

wednesday

○ Proteins ○ Carbs
○ Fruit & Veg ○ Fun

Snacks
_____
_____

Beverage
_____
_____

Rating ☆ ☆ ☆ ☆ ☆

lunch planner
FOR KIDS

thursday

- ○ Proteins   ○ Carbs
- ○ Fruit & Veg   ○ Fun

Snacks

Beverage

Rating ☆ ☆ ☆ ☆ ☆

friday

- ○ Proteins   ○ Carbs
- ○ Fruit & Veg   ○ Fun

Snacks

Beverage

Rating ☆ ☆ ☆ ☆ ☆

Favorites

Humm, please no more!

Weekly

monday

○ Proteins ○ Carbs
○ Fruit & Veg ○ Fun

Snacks
_____
_____

Beverage
_____
_____

Rating ☆ ☆ ☆ ☆ ☆

tuesday

○ Proteins ○ Carbs
○ Fruit & Veg ○ Fun

Snacks
_____
_____

Beverage
_____
_____

Rating ☆ ☆ ☆ ☆ ☆

wednesday

○ Proteins ○ Carbs
○ Fruit & Veg ○ Fun

Snacks
_____
_____

Beverage
_____
_____

Rating ☆ ☆ ☆ ☆ ☆

lunch planner
FOR KIDS

thursday

○ Proteins   ○ Carbs
○ Fruit & Veg   ○ Fun

Snacks
_____
_____

Beverage
_____
_____

Rating ☆ ☆ ☆ ☆ ☆

friday

○ Proteins   ○ Carbs
○ Fruit & Veg   ○ Fun

Snacks
_____
_____

Beverage
_____
_____

Rating ☆ ☆ ☆ ☆ ☆

Favorites

Humm, please no more!

Weekly

monday

○ Proteins   ○ Carbs
○ Fruit & Veg   ○ Fun

Snacks
_____
_____

Beverage
_____
_____

Rating ☆ ☆ ☆ ☆ ☆

tuesday

○ Proteins   ○ Carbs
○ Fruit & Veg   ○ Fun

Snacks
_____
_____

Beverage
_____
_____

Rating ☆ ☆ ☆ ☆ ☆

wednesday

○ Proteins   ○ Carbs
○ Fruit & Veg   ○ Fun

Snacks
_____
_____

Beverage
_____
_____

Rating ☆ ☆ ☆ ☆ ☆

lunch planner
FOR KIDS

thursday

○ Proteins   ○ Carbs
○ Fruit & Veg   ○ Fun

Snacks

Beverage

Rating ☆ ☆ ☆ ☆ ☆

friday

○ Proteins   ○ Carbs
○ Fruit & Veg   ○ Fun

Snacks

Beverage

Rating ☆ ☆ ☆ ☆ ☆

Favorites

Humm, please no more!

Weekly

monday

○ Proteins   ○ Carbs
○ Fruit & Veg   ○ Fun

Snacks
_____
_____

Beverage
_____
_____

Rating ☆☆☆☆☆

tuesday

○ Proteins   ○ Carbs
○ Fruit & Veg   ○ Fun

Snacks
_____
_____

Beverage
_____
_____

Rating ☆☆☆☆☆

wednesday

○ Proteins   ○ Carbs
○ Fruit & Veg   ○ Fun

Snacks
_____
_____

Beverage
_____
_____

Rating ☆☆☆☆☆

lunch planner
FOR KIDS

thursday

○ Proteins   ○ Carbs
○ Fruit & Veg   ○ Fun

Snacks

Beverage

Rating ☆☆☆☆☆

friday

○ Proteins   ○ Carbs
○ Fruit & Veg   ○ Fun

Snacks

Beverage

Rating ☆☆☆☆☆

Favorites

Humm, please no more!

Weekly

monday

○ Proteins   ○ Carbs
○ Fruit & Veg   ○ Fun

Snacks

Beverage

Rating ☆ ☆ ☆ ☆ ☆

tuesday

○ Proteins   ○ Carbs
○ Fruit & Veg   ○ Fun

Snacks

Beverage

Rating ☆ ☆ ☆ ☆ ☆

wednesday

○ Proteins   ○ Carbs
○ Fruit & Veg   ○ Fun

Snacks

Beverage

Rating ☆ ☆ ☆ ☆ ☆

lunch planner
FOR KIDS

thursday

○ Proteins   ○ Carbs
○ Fruit & Veg   ○ Fun

Snacks

Beverage

Rating ☆ ☆ ☆ ☆ ☆

friday

○ Proteins   ○ Carbs
○ Fruit & Veg   ○ Fun

Snacks

Beverage

Rating ☆ ☆ ☆ ☆ ☆

Favorites

Humm, please no more!

Weekly

monday

○ Proteins ○ Carbs
○ Fruit & Veg ○ Fun

Snacks
___
___

Beverage
___
___

Rating ☆ ☆ ☆ ☆ ☆

tuesday

○ Proteins ○ Carbs
○ Fruit & Veg ○ Fun

Snacks
___
___

Beverage
___
___

Rating ☆ ☆ ☆ ☆ ☆

wednesday

○ Proteins ○ Carbs
○ Fruit & Veg ○ Fun

Snacks
___
___

Beverage
___
___

Rating ☆ ☆ ☆ ☆ ☆

lunch planner
FOR KIDS

thursday

- ○ Proteins
- ○ Fruit & Veg
- ○ Carbs
- ○ Fun

Snacks

Beverage

Rating ☆☆☆☆☆

friday

- ○ Proteins
- ○ Fruit & Veg
- ○ Carbs
- ○ Fun

Snacks

Beverage

Rating ☆☆☆☆☆

Favorites

Humm, please no more!

Weekly

monday

○ Proteins ○ Carbs
○ Fruit & Veg ○ Fun

Snacks
_____
_____

Beverage
_____
_____

Rating ☆ ☆ ☆ ☆ ☆

tuesday

○ Proteins ○ Carbs
○ Fruit & Veg ○ Fun

Snacks
_____
_____

Beverage
_____
_____

Rating ☆ ☆ ☆ ☆ ☆

wednesday

○ Proteins ○ Carbs
○ Fruit & Veg ○ Fun

Snacks
_____
_____

Beverage
_____
_____

Rating ☆ ☆ ☆ ☆ ☆

lunch planner
FOR KIDS

thursday

○ Proteins   ○ Carbs
○ Fruit & Veg   ○ Fun

Snacks

Beverage

Rating ☆ ☆ ☆ ☆ ☆

friday

○ Proteins   ○ Carbs
○ Fruit & Veg   ○ Fun

Snacks

Beverage

Rating ☆ ☆ ☆ ☆ ☆

Favorites

Humm, please no more!

notes

notes

exclusive bonus

Download our interactive PDF grocery list.
Fill the pdf on your computer and print a clean list
or
print blank pages

Use this link : **www.ashleysnotebooks.com/grocery**

Made in the USA
Columbia, SC
30 March 2021